The Caprices

The Caprices
JAMES BYRNE

Arc PUBLICATIONS

2019

Published by Arc Publications
Nanholme Mill, Shaw Wood Road
Todmorden, OL14 6DA, UK
www.arcpublications.co.uk

Design by Tony Ward

978 1911469 85 8 (pbk)
978 1911469 86 5 (hbk)

Cover image:
'What a golden beak!' (aquatint 53)
from *Los Caprichos* by Francisco Goya

Editor for the UK & Ireland
John Wedgewood Clarke

Author's Acknowledgements

The *Los Caprichos* images which accompany these poems were originally published by Francisco Goya on February 6th, 1799. They are part of the original 'Prado' manuscript, republished by Dover Publications in 1969. Excerpts from this sequence first appeared in *Ambit*, *Buenos Aires Poetry*, *Blackbox Manifold*, *Granta*, *The Common*, *Long Poem Magazine*, *Morning Star*, *Poetry Review*, *Poetry Wales* and on University of Liverpool's 'Citizens of Everywhere' blog. The author is grateful to the editors of these publications. A brief selection also appeared in *Everything Broken Up Dances* (Tupelo Press, 2015).

The author would like to acknowledge the Academia in Madrid, Spain and the Ortiz Gallery in León, Nicaragua for their kindness in allowing access to original material.

Additional thanks are reserved for Edge Hill University, who gave the author a research grant to travel to Nicaragua to participate in the 13th Festival Internacional de Poesía de Granada Nicaragua in February 2017. Additional gratitude to Víctor Rodríguez Núñez and Kathleen Hedeen for translating some of these poems into Spanish. Also to Niall McDevitt, Sandeep Parmar and Julia Blackburn for their advice and readings of the manuscript.

And, of course, thanks to Goya himself.

Contents

Process notes: a dialogic ekphrasis with Goya

I first saw Francisco Goya's *Los Caprichos* at the Museum of Fine Arts in Boston, a few days before Christmas, 2014. Wanting to impress at an initial meeting with an art-savvy poetry editor, I was fortunate that my sister-in-law – then a Boston doctor – had membership of the gallery. She handed me a free pass which enabled me and the editor, Jim Schley of Tupelo, to gain entrance to the exhibition, which was enticingly entitled *Goya: Order and Disorder*. A generous retrospective of the Spanish master, divided into eight sections, the show promised an 'innovative approach' to the work, including themes that might be expected from any Goya exhibit, such as 'religious devotion and superstition'. But there were other, stranger curatorial headings like: 'nurturing and abuse of children' and 'justice gone awry'. They had the work he was most famous for: portraits from the Spanish court of King Ferdinand, some prints from *Los desastres de la guerra* (The Disasters of War) and portraits of Goya's aristocratic muse, the Duchess of Alba. Jim and I admired these. The technique is extraordinarily good – I would call him a proto-modernist or modern classicist. But the room we stayed in the longest, the one we couldn't bring ourselves to leave, included some fifteen or so etchings I'd heard about but never seen in the flesh: *Los Caprichos*. These eighty aquatint plates were probably etched between 1794 and 1798. They mark a distinct turning point in Goya's career and their publication almost cost him his life.

Though in his artistic prime, aged fifty-three, Goya had, only a few years earlier, survived a mysterious near-death experience. It has been suggested that this was Ménière's Disease, though it was probably something worse, perhaps even a complete psychological breakdown. Nobody knows, or nobody has told, quite what happened, but whatever the illness was it left Goya completely deaf and took him years to recover. Friends at the time thought he was lying on his deathbed. However, he slowly began, not just to paint again, but to read about the French Revolution, which was then at its most violent. Of particular interest to Goya was Jean-Jacques Rousseau's *Philosophie*, which he quotes in the most famous etching from the sequence, 'The Sleep of Reason Produces Monsters'.

It was daring for Goya, under the surveillance and patronage of the Spanish Court, to quote Rousseau, one of the leading radical French thinkers concerned with political and social inequalities. Spain was France's nervous neighbour at the end of the eighteenth century and its public inquisitions were intended to crush any social unrest or protest and, above all, to protect the monarchy, the ruling classes and the catholic church. Goya's *Caprichos* attack all of these things, in different ways, sometimes subtly, but often quite directly. Goya sympathises with the outsider figure, particularly women, who are often courted by leering aristocrats. The powerful appear as devils. Doctors are donkeys. Duchesses witches. A lecturer, speaking from a pulpit, transforms into a talking parrot. This, of course, invokes the fantastical and satiric, but *Los Caprichos* are also serious and subversive. *Caprichos* 23 and 24 ('Those specks of dust' and 'Nothing could be done about it') feature two figures, wrists bound, wearing their mark of shame: the inquisitional dunce's hat.

Criticising the inquisition in Spain was as good as signing your own death warrant and Goya was lucky to survive the 1799 publication of the prints. They were available to the public for four years before the King, who was said to have liked Goya personally, asked him to hand over all the unsold copies and, quite amazingly, took responsibility for protecting the artist by pretending the monarchy had, in fact, commissioned them. Perhaps this also allowed

King Ferdinand to smother the subversive power of the work by claiming ownership, finally censoring the prints. Whatever happened in the bargain made between painter and monarch, Goya managed, in giving the prints over to the Crown, to barter a large enough sale price to ensure that his son, Javier, received a large pension.

Los Caprichos. The Caprices. Caprice as in faddish impulsion, foolery or whim. Don't be fooled. There's nothing whimsical about these prints. There's a ludic and vatic sensibility at work, often simultaneously. Sometimes playfulness is the vision itself. Though, as in the poetry that has always appealed to me most, mere play is insufficient for Goya. Any satiric impulse behind these prints usually is transformed into something more sinister. Goya's grisly cast are metamorphic, based on real characters, *seen* as imagination, which involves its own castings and metaphors. Goya is interested in the narratives of power: who has it, how it is enacted, who suffers, who serves up the cruelty. Obviously, this is relevant for our age (or any age) in the everness of violence, crookedness, struggle. Caprice echoes capriciousness and the wicked, as so often today, are also the empowered, enacting their power over women, children, the poor, even the elderly. Goya, in reflecting the violence and struggles of Europe at a time of political and social revolution, is obsessed with the terror of power and appoints a ghastly series of caricatures to make his point.

After a few hours in the exhibition, Jim and I went outside with a headful of Goya terror. He wanted to go through a poetry manuscript of mine, which had been accepted for publication. We sat outside in the snow on a freezing cold bench and, though it wasn't suggested, I realised that the book we were discussing would be incomplete without some kind of response to *Los Caprichos*. "Write them all for your next book" was the advice given. But days later I asked Jim to keep the door open for an initial series to be published in *Everything Broken Up Dances*, which he kindly agreed to do.

At that point, I wondered which poets had written about *Los Caprichos*. Before I left Boston I bought a collection by Jerome Rothenberg. Influence (as if without us) attempts the synchronic and Rothenberg sought to prove this, as my hand fell open on a scattering of poems he had written loosely following *Los Caprichos*. Perhaps there were other poets. I faintly remembered that Ted Hughes had tried out a few 'Caprice' poems before abandoning them. Part of me didn't want to know or find out in case it interrupted my will to write the book. Besides, my stubborn nerve was convinced that I could do something different anyway.

Writing up the first ten of Goya's aquatints from the slightly foggy 1969 Dover Publications reprint of the original Prado manuscript – a book I carried everywhere with me – my first responses took the form of octaves and were written in fairly conventional rhyme, something that I had refused over the previous decade. Subliminally, I was probably influenced by the form of the plates themselves. Perhaps in 'plating' the poems I felt I was opening a further dialogue with Goya as much as writing a straightforward ekphrastic response or deviating from the material too far.

Dialogo in Spanish means a conversation or a dialogue but also relates to, or speaks of, negotiations and, of course logos / language. Everything I write is a conversation, a dialogue of some kind. Writing, for me, has always been both solitary and communal. Often Goya would start the conversation and I would pitch a response. Sometimes I wanted to stay fairly faithful to the source image, but more often than not it involved a drifting or – as the Spanish say – a *deriva* (to drift or be adrift) from the source material. Looking at the poems again now, I notice they inevitably include a lot of what was happening to me or newsflashes seen during the time I wrote them. However, in each of my

14

responses, something of the original remains, sufficient for me to publish the poems with Goya's images underneath, so as to reflect distances as much as semblances.

Following the structure of the Prado manuscript, sometimes the etching itself wasn't the main focus. This manuscript includes wonderful, sometimes poetry-rich short texts which were also written by Goya and translated by Hilda Harris in 1964. Occasionally, as noted at the end of this book, I echo or correspond with these as much as the images themselves. For example, in *Los Caprichos* 6, the text mentions 'Face, dress and voice, are all false' which appears similarly in the opening two lines of my poem:

> Wear a face to look more like yourself.
> Clothes, flesh and voice are all false.

For years I have written and taught within or around the idea of ekphrastic poetry. Ekphrasis (literarily 'out-speak', nowadays meaning how one art corresponds with another) goes back to Homer and his depiction of the shield of Achilles. Various writers on ekphrasis – I think of John Hollander and Alfred Corn – advise that the poem should stand alone from the original material or, as Corn suggests, seek to 'confront' the visual image. But this sounds too aggressive to me. I prefer something active – or, better, activist, still ekphrastic in its approach perhaps, but also giving echolalic credence to the channels of correspondence. Charles Bernstein recently used the term 'echopoetics' and I would like to apply it in relation to my concept of dialogic ekphrasis. Is it more difficult to echo the dead? With Goya, I found that there was not so much a liking of the work that made me want to write about it – though I think these etchings extraordinary – more a haunting. The process was as much physical as visual in the sense that I would look at one of his *Caprichos* in the morning, usually before teaching at university, allow it to filter, disturb or settle through me and then, by the end of the day, write up the octave, reflecting on the original image while filling it with further echoes from the day itself.

By the time I'd written beyond the selection in *Everything Broken Up Dances*, my process was interrupted, partly by teaching, but also because of a desire to visit Goya's Spain. I wanted to see what effect Madrid's streets where he created *Los Caprichos* would have on my poetics. Also, I hoped to look at an original copy of the rare Prado manuscript and had emailed before visiting to announce my interest. No reply. So when I arrived in Madrid in June 2016, I went straight to the museum and was promptly told *Los Caprichos* weren't on display. The guide recommended the nearby Academia instead, a far smaller museum and once Spain's most prestigious art school – the place where Goya had twice failed to be admitted as a student, that is, until he got in with the King and was given the equivalent of honorary membership. Two great things happened there. Firstly, The Academia were exhibiting the original engraved plates, some fifteen of them (apparently they change the selection every five years). New detail abounded that simply wasn't there in the Prado manuscript. Each plate was wreathed with previously unseen lines. Colours were reversed. White became black, black white (an example of this is in 'And so was his grandfather' on p. 60). Oddly symbolic gestures like a hidden masonic crest or a background demon appeared and I chose to include some of these surprises, though not all.

On my last afternoon in Madrid I stayed in the Academia until it closed and filled up my notebook. I had the room to myself for an hour but for a lovey-dovey couple who peered into the exhibition, curious then horrified. For some ten minutes, a cravated man (a rival poet?) came in and began filling up his notebook. I remember how we scraped elbows trying to write up *Caprichos* 53. At around 5 pm a burly security guard was following me around the room rattling his keys. A door opened and another member of staff passed through and, to break the ice with a joke – because I knew it was impossible – I asked her if there was any way I might hold one of the plates. She laughed but said they had a rare manuscript I could look at right away. The backroom office was open for another half an hour. Within a few minutes I was sitting at a desk frantically fingering through Juan Agustin Cean Bermudez's own copy of the *Caprichos* with gloved hands. I asked for a selection (plates 40-55) which bore the Spanish critic and personal friend of Goya's own captions written in Spanish. This felt like a major discovery. I made quick impromptu notes and some of these seeped into the final versions. Even Bermudez's Spanish felt foreboding and allowed for a more bilingual writing of the text (*'pinta un gorilla'* in *Caprichos* 41). Sometimes I have included the Spanish without translating it, just fitting the language into an existing impression, sonic effect or narrative.

A second, unexpected encounter with *Los Caprichos* occurred during my visit to read at a poetry festival in Granada, Nicaragua in 2017. At this point, I had about ten octaves left to write for the original draft of the book. A friend at the festival, the Dutch artist and writer Bas Kwakman, had just returned from León. "There are some Goyas you might be interested in" said Bas. I anticipated a selection of the courtly portraits, perhaps a couple of prints, but when I arrived to the hush of the Ortiz Gallery in León, I found an entire set of the *Caprichos*, which included a second manuscript belonging to Salvador Dalí, who had drawn, graffiti-like, over the original prints. Though I encountered an entire set of the prints again in 2018, in Zaragoza, a city near Goya's birthplace, the León experience was a key moment of fortuity, as pleasurable as any experience I've ever had as a poet.

Goya's *Los Caprichos* are a series of real-life nightmares that haunt the twenty-first century. Responding to some of these, this book was written during times of increased polarisation in Europe, when political events like BREXIT were painfully debated (my version of 'The Sleep of Reason...' beginning "Now that the State legitimises hate..." was written on the day of Britain's EU referendum); when Donald Trump ('clownstick') began to gain political traction in the US polls and came out winning with his tales of 'fake news'; when a man mowed down a Bastille Day crowd in Nice and a hundred children died in one week in Aleppo. Even Harvey Weinstein ('cocksnook') makes an appearance amid several other poems that offer solidarity with the #MeToo movement, written against the continued exploitation of women in the twenty-first century.

Arguably, the world we live in today is more terrifying than Goya's Spain because – in over two hundred years since he created *Los Caprichos* – we have become more cool about human inhumanity. The echo grows louder, the world becomes more absurd, more criminal and yet, perversely, our collective response all too often verges on the whimsical. Goya, echoing in his deafness, hears our own, capturing all these elements variously throughout his masterwork.

James Byrne

por ti enciendo mi incesario.

Por ti, cuya gran paleta,
caprichosa, brusca, inquieta.

*

for you I light fragrant incense.

To the greatness of your palette
that's capricious, brash, incited.

RUBEN DARIO, 'To Goya'

Francisco Goya y Lucientes, Pintor

You cannot condone this. Your face
tired of pleasantry, shatters the dark.
You add a self-portrait to save face,
kiss the hand of the king for a sack
of gold, for Javier who will not visit.
Awake! Old man, deaf on The Street
of Dissolution; a city's floodgate
in your caved ears, the swelling tide.

They say yes and give their hand to the first comer

For whom the story does not end well
is not liberated. Swooned to man,
blind on entering the masked ball
that is marriage. Dark suitors among
the packrat crowd. One foot points
towards an illegitimate altar, the other
heeled, but offering no resistance.
Complicit is she who would not demur.

El si pronuncian y la mano alargan
Al primero que llega.

Here comes the bogeyman

To summon a father from the shit
of roots and odours. *Abuso funesto.*
Call him by names that do not exist,
he follows you like a sun's shadow.
The annex of his echo is sanguinary
and a pricked finger tastes of his blood.
Fathers and sons become men of rivalry,
boys cannot know beyond their good.

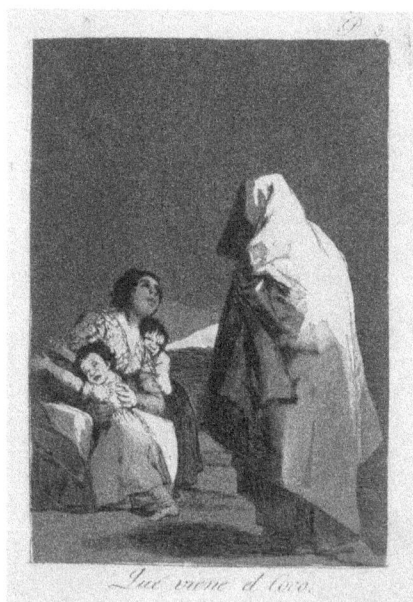

Que viene el coco.

Nanny's Boy

Snug-ugly, raised on nanny's hams,
made of eyes so as not to see sense.
Grown insufferable, child as man,
carousing in drag on stag weekends.
If family is the world's first true woe,
it is followed by the family corrupted.
Play piggywiggy with him, let him go
to the market to find himself, she said.

El de la rollona

Two of a kind

Enkindled: one loves as the other,
is as vile as the other. The coxcomb's
limp grin turns the Duchess of Alba,
five years shy of her widowy frown.
Synchronised clocks of their faces,
hands timed to the geomagnetic field.
Who can legislate for attractiveness?
Who knows as another person feels?

Tal para qual

Nobody knows himself

Wear a face to look more like yourself.
Clothes, flesh and voice are all false.
I am the mystery, occasioned as myself,
compound volatile, sewn at the mouth.
Look me in the eye and I am elsewhere,
I sleep, silent as ink. Ancestral breath
blows clean the curtain. Dreams are
embroidered from people that exist.

Even thus he cannot make her out

Love evolves despite the shadows
of desire. Bane of Aristotle's *akrasia*,
scythe to the tree, power's erogenous
will *vs* nature. The monocle glowers.
The man stooped at her shoulder, as if
from constipation. A rake, a crooner,
inimitably flirtatious. Love sings us
mysterious, is both *favola* and *musica*.

¿Ni asi la distingue

They carried her off

Anjashna, who are the they is he
and is you: possessors enact their law.
Woman as cargo glass. *La muger qe
no se sabe guardar.* Man is impure
as the dirt he would taint you with.
Before the schoolgirls in Chibok
were carried off to Sambisa forest,
all those wearing trousers were shot.

Que se la llevaron!

Tantalus

Wake me up when it is all over.
Like a bad dub in the demo studio,
only your voice is ever really there.
Dispassionate in *sotto voce*, Tantalo,
rumouring with grubbers at the market,
yet so cold as to make stew of his son.
Plead with the gods, the tantalising light,
the shadow weight of sky across a tomb.

Tantalo.

Love and Death

The mind spars like darkness inside
a lighthouse. A battery field flashes,
a corporal laughs at the undrawn sword
and the corpse that has begun to speak
through me drinks the breath from
my mouth. Hold me, closer, the world
outside falls to pieces between men.
We live, divisible, as if on a threshold.

El amor y la muerte

Lads making ready

Skeletally regressed, frowns for eyes,
mouthing off the national notionals.
Lunks on the Hooligan Express line,
making ready, as if for a clarion call.
To be afire in the flamecasing of war.
Lied to, but neverminding, you inscape,
sharpen, wait like shrapnel in the air.
There is always someone else to hate.

Muchachos al avío.

Out hunting for teeth

Calderon's cauldron stirs blood.
Red moon, black star, she turns
her face away to pluck the hind
teeth of a hanged man. Efficacious,
not sorcerer, not woman, but each
as othered, someone fleered on the
scaffold block as a common witch,
then carted to the disasters of war.

A caza de dientes.

They are hot

The television chef is hungrier than soil.
In the vibrating darkness of my house,
he feeds me food as something spectral
but physical, like anxiety. He's the proof
of stiffy puddings, the coenocyte gullet,
consumptive as self-immolation or glut.
You turn up the fire for a kitchen's heat,
live for the meals you've not been fed.

Están calientes

What a sacrifice

At the cost of freedom unhappy,
metaphor is design without you.
The auntie trembles herself to sleep
like a lark panicked in a hedgerow.
Sound of a hi-hat playing snares.
Chosen from photographs and bank
balances, a list of listless strangers.
Her father stares through his hand.

Que sacrificio!

Pretty teachings

She overstood. She shadowiest. She
kindcold deuce, headless in distance.
Who wrangles with the shade of a tree
is silent as a warship on the docks.
Speech like a moth in the ear. Advice
worthy as a giver whose letter is deferred.
What kind of sky is this when the stars
connive above and cannot shoot straight?

Bellos consejos

For heaven's sake: and it was her mother

Look away long enough and these clouds
will pass to the south. Home was a place
I had to hide in, patient as a chrysalis.
For years, I dug the earth to make sense
of what I might endure or tunnel out
from. Not restored but marked, awkward.
To live without is to be pursued. Night
after night, I swim in your hood of mud.

Dios la perdone: Y era su madre.

It is nicely stretched

Oh! La tia curra... she is no fool.
Familiar as a scar, wound to zero,
to squat below the girl from a stool.
Willed antinomy, love the first to go
in a rival's synthesis. Blood icing
into frost. The younger interned
by the bed's shadow peels stockings
from a thin leg, waits another turn.

Bien tirada está.

And his house is on fire

You talk and talk but say nothing.
Candle into fire. Bad wine burling
around the brain, dismissing everything
but substance, the union of thinking.
Come out from the coffin shop of the id.
All experience means to cross danger.
Your house is in flames and you do not
know it. You stare and stare into the fire.

Yiole quema la Casa

All will fall

Those who have sinned fall shortest.
A child in the sky flew querulous,
was felled by the hand of a satirist.
Like Icarus in labyrinths of Daedalus,
or the frizzy Duchess, fabulously rich,
not sitting against Franco's fascism
for Picasso, but with a matador naked.
Mytho-cryptic, life is euhemerism.

There they go plucked

Shoo the bird with a heavy broom.
The world would pluck its feathers
on a slab. Tired of circadian rhythm,
Oedipus crawls, childlike on all fours,
searching for Laius in the white sky.
Amorist son, shiest among mothers,
be quiet as the waterfowl that lies
wrapped in the down of a comforter.

Ya van desplumados.

How they pluck her

What succours the lion? Prey lain
bare as fishes. Enzymes of saliva
via the perfumed strutting of a hen.
One offending word shatters the air
and diminishes the gaming reserve
of language. Utterance disaffirmed
for fetching and gathering. A word
resounds like a cry inside a wood.

¡Qual la descañonan!

Poor little girls

Arrival of those who are freighted in.
Who are decided upon. Passion gives
passage. Bari docks ship women
to arrive incognito, by night, for lives
pimped to college boy and pisshead.
Grief's appal, you shuffle behind her,
weighing kilo to debt, flesh as object,
mother's voice cloying at your ear.

Pobrecitas!

Those specks of dust

Taunt the honourable with catcalls.
Fan the flames of inquisition. They
bow a head to boulevard whistles.
Fifth Avenue's cold sun of memory
whispers for them a name that ladies
only speak unspoken. Whose shame
is this, worn longer than acridities,
passing heckles? The crowd's a djinn.

Aquellos polbos.

Nothing could be done about it

Like a lancer in the backcloth,
you act up by doing nothing. Again,
shame! Bound to fuel the hoarded lot
into a gallery of swingers at Tyburn.
Boredom. Flashbulb. Distraction,
yet your roots still pant with blood.
You decide: humility or humiliation.
A donkey honk of shit, or of pride.

¿ No hubo remedio.

Yes he broke the pot

So come the thrashings of rod or clog.
So temper only breeds more mischief.
Dash the boy like a blind man would
key Braille. Tell him the story of himself.
Audacity strikes at the lake. The wing
of a goose gongs the water. Tell the child
it is a matter of weight in air. Air sung
alive to the ear that listens, and is mild.

Si quebró el Cantaro.

They've already got a seat

Pleased at his invitation to be seated,
she smiles for him, balancing a chair
on her head. Obedience is seatedness.
She is quiet at the clownstick laughter
of the vulgarian. How to contravene
the speaking of silence into speech
when put upon or tended like a garden?
Her bare legs brighten up the dress.

Ya tienen asiento.

Which of them is more overcome?

Societal lust. Practical measures over
abstract concepts. Levelled compasses
over ethics. Bowing from a black four-
-in-hand, the young charlatan, half death,
half doomed young, feigns the honouring
of a dance card. A tango with a Duchess
counts for money well spent, he thinks.
Same as the other. Two poodles in a tryst.

Quien mas rendido?

Hush

Not for all the secrecies of Venus
would she collude with Hippomenes.
No gold apple stirs the translucence
between her eyes, chalky with mist.
Gossip shared disturbs an ocean,
scallops whiteness from the star.
Blabbermouth prattles on and on,
scandalising the flaws of her sister.

Chiton.

That certainly is being able to read

Combing Sunday nibs for a headline.
The loss of language ages us, Eduard.
Schizophrene grief on losing Einstein,
a family smithereened to its heart.
Albert exiled to the Olsonian lectern
on Black Mountain. Tete in Burgholzli,
alone, enwalled, shocked as Bedlam.
Black is the scent of electricity.

Why hide them?

To avarice pocketing a pouch sack.
To treasuries buried under numerals.
Money disappears into haircracks
like a lizard scuttling into a wall.
Old man, face wracked by the sea,
buried under this Great Depression.
Living alack, what's owed is illusory.
The banker smirks like a sovereign.

Porque esconderlos?

She prays for her

Motherbride, who art in heaven,
who wills her through the narrows
of the Calle Isobel, its daily attrition
of untouched staring. Pray a hare's
-foot, that she might wideawake
as the surgeon who spares a wound.
Hallowed flesh that is beyond luck.
A single prayer beaded from sound.

Ruega por ella.

Because she was susceptible

What is mistook is taken. Captive
under the interrogation of lamplight,
in Caballero Garcia's siffle of piss,
a nameless girl, gangrenous, bleached
white. Arise, oma, ummi, to give birth
on the Avenida del Prado (is it a boy?).
Velázquez's buffoon son, Calabacillas.
Life conspires. There is no other way.

Por que fue sensible.

To the Count Palatine or the Count of the Palate

Kingsize, the palatium is sick. Ask
chamberlains for a whiff of the royal
shitstink. Unstabled equerries yack
lethal cocktails into calfskin sandals
after grooming for African vectors.
Citizens subjected to a master who,
in promising nothing, accomplishes
everything. To stoop is to bend low.

Sleep overcomes them

Perchance happiness hooded in
sleep. A ventilated tunnel hutch
where I shy from the vexed orison
of consciousness. Pallid thought
cast in a red dye of remembrance
then swarmed as a gossip's hive.
Age wretches. Calamity scorns
the life alive that is born to live.

Las rinde el Sueño.

She fleeces him

Tonsorial stead of the barbette,
a barb on the flame of Miss Lovett.
Stray hands under a ruffled dress,
chop sidewhiskers, slit a throat.
Lucy with a bore-honed open razor,
hacks back at Sweeney's mytheme.
Seated over fate's shadowy trapdoor,
to be cooked into a gristly meat pie.

Le desnuñona

A bad night

Remember the roly-poly grinner
behind Marilyn's wind-frilled dress?
Recast him into the dark exposure
like a threat in the air, as in Goya's
'Mala Noche' where nighthawks squall
shame upon the gallivant. Your guilt,
Pintor, your flint stare, your domicile.
Josefa, only she can reclaim this night.

Might not the pupil know more?

Professor Equus is an ass. Algebraic
seriousness (and as formulaic). What
can he teach beyond the hologrammic
surface of curricula? Knockoff shop
of antiquity where you enter as idea
then participant. Gigabyte memory,
Wikipedia clutched like a bannister.
Greyscale wallpaper in the library.

Bravo!

At the festival of silence, I applaud
from within my anechoic chamber.
Papier-mâché symphonies, a Galliard
triple-step between lady and courtier.
No matter of the Nonet instrumental,
or the musical tunefulness of a word.
The artist listens loudest to council
patronage. What is spoken is unheard.

Brabisimo

And so was his grandfather

Mad with heralds in the *aguafuerte*.
Dressage after dressage of horses
whitewash the scrapbook of history.
Darwinist cagebirds, hidden crests
sing to an ear black with deafness.
Genealogy tracts extract ancestral
war. Estranger danger. Whiteness,
it's the deadliest colour of them all.

Of what ill will he die?

Bathe him in *abuelo*'s shadows.
Fire the heart's eye as it closes.
The doctor, attending, only knows
the study of his own pensiveness,
not the east wind feathering death.
A lit kiln already cooks for him
to burn in the family photograph.
It's the last image of imagination.

De que mal morira?

Neither more nor less

Self others you as someone else.
Metamorphia of Wilde's Dorian,
the man who rode his own hearse.
Pinta un gorilla. Human revision.
The ass's face mutates a canvas,
is brushed into life by a monkey.
Portrait in a gallery of aristocrats,
the likeness distorts like money.

Thou who canst not

As if the weight that we carried
were love, not a pocket of silver.
Bloodshadow rivers in white sand,
is whispered at the buccaneer's ear
by King Ferdinand. Eighty Maravedis
for the price of a cavalry, a peninsula.
On their backs, the sign of the beast,
the profiteer that relies on war.

The sleep of reason produces monsters

Now that the state legitimises hate,
a wakeful trump of doom thunders
valley deep (where are the Blake's
and Miltons now?). Crisis of mirrors
where my neighbour reasons only
with himself: a hissing face, chained
to sleep in a star's coda. A fantasy,
that whatever is pure is ENGLAND.

They spin finely

Knife-light shrouded like darkness
inside a cloud. Medea in *aquatinta*,
more bacchant than parent. Eyeless,
benumb with ritual odium, *y la trama*
unwarps, hibble to hex, spins a thread
as the devil weaves, severs the heart
from its home. To every child denied
love: cut familial strings, find an EXIT.

Hilan delgado

There is plenty to suck

Snuffbox laughter. Baby cradles.
Our mouths shudder open and shut.
Ladling out hell's hot audacities,
joy blooded to the shadow of a bat.
Meritocratic suck and substance
fortifies the consumable boomer.
My name is he who supplants,
unsupplanted by the supplanter.

Mucho hay que chupar

Correction

Corrected by inquisitional crosses,
the Barahona witches were forced
to stick their heads into carved holes
of rock called The Confessional Post.
Dies Irae. A judgment so hymnal,
the wigged gentleman turns away,
docile with censure, ever-faithful,
he prays to his voyeur in the sky.

Corrección

A gift for the master

Don't call me Sir, I'm a worker too.
Grand Dame, Grandee, all hierarchy
is diabolical. Panoptic subterfuge,
where the eye opens perpetually
on Sisyphus pushing a hulk of rock
downhill. The drudger is never
less than the master and all work
preserves the burden of labour.

Obsequio á el maestro

Tale-bearers – Blasts of wind

Knowing is not to blast on about it.
Cover your ears to the taxidermal
tale-bearer retweeting the internet.
Faux messiah, you heard the call
to a calling only to create yourself
from an irate, offstage understudy.
If anyone ever knew themselves
they'd be silent as *Śākyamuni*.

Hobgoblins

Another kind of people hobgoblins
the minds of little men. No Bunyan
fiend is he who frightens a maiden
of ancient privilege. Happy as no-one
but a freak. Hand of Puck who jokes
sweetly unfree to sweeten a Dukedom.
The wrong face in the oldest village
is another's. A goblin is no Athenian.

Duendecitos

The Chinchillas

Hear nothing. Know nothing. Good
for nothing (welcome to the family).
Padlocks for ears, a mouth spoonfed
by the devil's ass. Tired of history,
Frankenstein yowls the forest down;
Lear on the heath like a chessboard
missing its king. Spit fire, spout rain.
A mouth opens, swallows the world.

Los Chinchillas.

They spruce themselves up

Mirror-rapid, fashion's equivocalness
lies in a killing of the ideal image.
Configured, as if through looking glass,
terror's flaw lives under a human face
and all error a pernicious business. God
of uniform discord, let me sleep awhile
in Loki's shadow, on Naglfar's boat,
its hull made of hair and fingernails.

Se repulen

What a tailor can do!

The eye torn blind by appearances.
The eye skiffling the light of prayer.
Cataract misfocus of a pale mother's
wet black eye. In coral faces I saw her,
questioning every blue-eyed nobility,
studying the world, its cloud garlands.
Eye that sees more than it wants to see;
a hooded man with stumps for arms.

Lo que puede un Sastre!

What a golden beak!

A bird's eye so vivid it cannot think
of you or I, or beyond what is seen.
When it speaks the sound of a syrinx
tightens around a catapult-shaped bone.
Beware of false prophets at the pulpit.
Bittacus's talk is all cheap cheap cheap.
The church fills like a mouth yet the sick
still huddle round for something to eat.

Que pico de Oro!

The shamefaced one

For shame to wear a face is shame
on you. Sneer in the pollenate dark,
shake an elliptical fist, find a name
for ash hungering the dust. Mark's
command of civic duty – the lover
as thy neighbour as thyself. Citizen
who shames me, whose hands are
covered with the blood of the sun.

Until death

Mirror mirrors queen and spinster.
Death as complexion. Skin's obelisk
shatters like fire and the prettier titter
like *prettig* (cunning) or *prettr* (trick).
Arsonists at the candling of birthdays,
thorns in the aureole, you will not die
standing up for something, as the trees
do, as she who is *la madre de la muerte*.

To rise and fall

Mistreated, he would subtend the sun.
Trick of axis. Gravity's blackest hole –
breath becoming thought, ambition.
He simply wanted to change the world
into himself. Coleridge called it egoana.
How the braggadocio likes to step on
your shoulders. Mad inside its own law,
the avalanche that rises before falling.

Subir y bajar.

The Filiation

Yes, foolery of the ledger, but Goya
fouls the fairer gender. Wake him away
from courtly matriarchies. It is her
sufferance in the marriage of pedigree
arranged by duty; her Honours degree
stirring a skillet for the new Master.
Incompetent, thick as mother's ghee,
he checks balances of land and ledger.

La filiación

Swallow it, dog

Name? Interrogation's blackest sun.
Age? Old as vexation. Address? Fire
ash of moon. Hot schist of mountain.
Why are you here? Vertigo as desire.
Excess of loneliness. Death's syringe.
What do you see when you look at us?
Bone-light behind the eyes. Swinge
of terror's lance. A man on his knees.

And still they don't go!

Calais wears the snakefoot of Boreas.
Coldest wind, nebular wind. Temper
of a falling wall. Calais dehumanises us
from they, flesh from flesh. The hunter
gathers her to go, but where? No Zephyr
in the West, no water in this jungle.
The boy inside a shipping container
holds up a picture of his dead uncle.

Y aun no se van!

Trials

Pick his brain to find the motherlode
of the bomb. The skull's pitch is a mine
of information. Goya trials the He-Goat,
unblinking, apocryphal, but real as one
of Bulgakov's Beelzebubs. His shadow
cat stalks inside the theatre of the mind,
estuarial as revelation. All that I know
is hauled, as if by a hand inside my head.

Ensayos.

They have flown

Peril she who flies on the public pedestal.
All politico is a headful of flammable gas.
The rustbelt of a mouth speaks, the citadel
runs her Learjet aground. Haynish voices
inebriant at the stump rally. Market forces
assume crash position, knowing that man /
woman, like the world at large, undresses
itself in the dark. What cannot fly is flown.

Volaverunt

Who would have thought it!

In the *auri sacra fames* he befriends
his enemy as accomplice. Who would
have thought it, a majority, tyrannous,
to tear the hair from our heads? Lord
Mogul cashes in on the intermezzo,
nods to the stage that was lain for him
by aristocrats of Mandarin and Rome.
Dutiful spirit in the spirit of capitalism.

¿Quién lo creyera?

Look how solemn they are!

Choose not I or you but she with him.
Hollywood likes it under a barcode sky
best of all [insert possessive pronoun
here]. Raptorial cackle. The predatory
cocksnook squats on her back. The sun
says nothing, sinking into a white cloud
made of bone. Her tells her, tell no-one.
If you are my friend, I am your friend.

Miren que grabes

Bon Voyage

If light thinks of time, darkness is time
thinking about itself. Black butterfly,
fly the diaphanousness of this wind,
exhume the moon, syllabise the sky.
I know of how but not where to live.
The resident alien cannot build a home,
the orphan waits outside the orphanage.
At night, she likes to sleep with a light on.

.Buen Viage.

Where is mother going?

Plant a handstand and shake your tush
on the dance floor (yes, all mothers can
get carried away). Devotion broods lust
and everyone, at one time, likes being
held by the devil's henchmen. In his eyes
(and his, his) she stares the distance down,
less a mother, more one of Botticelli's
cherubs. Men love that kind of thing.

¿Donde vá mamá?

There it goes

In the burden service of national causes,
you let the fatcat hitch a ride on the arm
of your crutches. Above all, to be of use,
to swear their downcast countenances in,
as if proscribing sickness from medicine.
Murder's laughter from airport to border,
where you fly blind, like a bat flapping
at echoes. Easy prey for the fearmonger.

Allá vá eso.

Wait 'til you've been anointed

What's realisable in this sky? I'm rooted
to face value like a clown without makeup.
I cannot stroll in the park, half-anointed
by thought, without some local schmuck
playing the latest dubstep on his phone.
If spoken to, I avert my eyes and, if pressed,
I hand over the ration slip of laconicism.
Debarred, held down, waiting on my health

¿Aguarda que te untan?

Pretty teacher

Teach me to sing your skin's music.
Black orchard of hair on my shoulder,
a thin hand silking the nape of my neck.
Is it touch or pulse or something closer
than either? (Loy called it electrolife).
How an owl's vigilance wakes the nest
of my sleep. How I know you as flight
and have only flown because you exist.

Linda maestra

Blow

The fire from your arse could light
a meteorite, boy. Pray on the gospel
for an audience of catacombs. At best
be seen and not heard upon the idol's
winged cry and know your torturer
from your history. Living is gaseous.
Fake news. Criminality of the law.
Who is that man tearing at my flesh?

Devout Profession

Maestras. Superiores. I have obeyed,
have swept, have sucked, have washed
your garret floors and pillowed quiet
the yelling of my sisters, but for what?
To be arranged and measured by a pair
of shadow-mouthed ecclesiasts. Men
who insist on scripture after scripture.
These pages are not written by women.

Devota profesion.

When day breaks we will be off

That the stars could be tissue paper
or, better, coated in sugar, she says,
and points, blind, a bony forefinger
to the nowhere sky of Europe; place
displacing her, a woman suppliant,
as in Aeschylus, counting on familiars,
like friendliness. Why is it in this land
they look at me like we are strangers?

You will not escape

Catch me if you can, kiss me quick.
Dali's graffitio strings her literally,
hand to foot (call him a surrealist?).
Avida's Dollars, but for Goya isn't she
strung up enough? Beaked attention,
of crag-faced men. A wizened owl
looks down on her, feigns wisdom.
The sneering ignorance of his scowl.

¿No te escaparás

It is better to be lazy

Work asides the important business
of doing something else. Call it ennui
not laziness, to stare into the endless
depths of a horizon. Some would say
working is violence (no other animal
is forced to do it). In the loneliness
between her arms, Dali adds a skull.
The crone laughs into a sweaty cuff.

Don't scream, stupid

As if Sod's law passed a new order.
Poor Paquilla, frozen as a puppet.
She walks the liminal road in her
tawdry wedding gown only to meet
Martinico, a levitational goblin and
an unnamed dwarf gnome hovering
behind her. Eyes to camera for a cut,
but the picture just keeps spooling.

No grites, tonta).

Can't anyone untie us?

What's missing from her hand?
The sour apple of Eden. Or so Dali
would have it, gouging out the eyes
of the blue devil that squats each
night on their bed. Rooted as a tree
struggling in wind. What's missing,
Avida? An island to flesh the corniche.
A love that stands against falling.

¿No hay quien nos desate?

You understand?... well, as I say...

Servility of canes on which an empire
rests heavy. Eyes of onyx stone, cockade
of the walk, he limps on proudly as war,
checking every face along the parade
for poisoners in the mob, gastric flabs
swilling off sugar-looted rum. In later
life, a gouty Columbus bled from the eyes.
¡Desgraciado Almirante! Sangre y ceniza.

What one does to another

It's fortune's caprice that kills us off.
Yesterday he was the gorging bull;
today, a ghostface haunting the plazas.
The judge who sided against the huddle.
The barrister who counted his clients like
coins in a drawer. Look at them now,
Judases, Cains, every possession knap-
sacked, but with nowhere left to go.

Unos à otros.

Be quick, they are waking up

What is the devil if not someone
who would wring a dove? Who does
everything for nothing and then some.
Ask monkeybrain; his hand flanks
the bird's feathery crop like terror
waking up. Entire days pass like this,
one simply sweeps over the other.
Every morning I wash off the grease.

Despacha que despiertan

No one has seen us

A bilious hiccough rises from the cellar.
A mouth closes, toothless, black as burial.
[Hic]. Knock back another, pour another,
until the last glass shatters the barrel, until
you are served, gurgling the wine darkness
of your shadow. Here's a toast. To unhealth.
To the spooks. [Hic, Hic]. Swig on this.
Feast of the Furies. The last of your breath.

Nadie nos ha visto.

It is time

With a grimace then, to go without
inhaling the sun. But I served my time,
I swallowed the jailor's key in my mouth.
Now the fire sign rises, it's only old men
who shriek in the flames. I'm not like them.
When I close my eyes they open on you,
bright in the Puerta del Sol. Bell chimes.
Ten in the morning. *Silencio. Silencio...*

Notes

pp. 7-9 – In the Contents (and throughout this book), the titles are from the original 'Prado' manuscript, reprinted and translated in *Los Caprichos*, Dover Editions, 1969. The author uses occasional words and phrases from the Prado 'captions', first translated by Hilda Harris in 1964, in some cases retaining the original Spanish. Not all of these are mentioned below.

p. 19 – This is an extract from Ruben Dario's poem 'To Goya', published in *Ruben Dario: Selected Writings*, Penguin Classics (US), 2005, Edited with an Introduction by Ilan Stavans and translated by Greg Simon & Steven F. White.

p. 28 – *'Even thus he cannot make her out'*: 'akrasia' is Aristotle's term pertaining to weakness of will. A phrase played on at the end of this section is *'favola in musica'*, a seventeenth-century term meaning 'story in music'.

p. 29 – *'They carried her off'*: *'La muger qe no se sabe guardar'* is from the caption text of the Prado manuscript and roughly translates as 'the woman who cannot take care of herself'.

p. 38 – *'It is nicely stretched'*: *'Oh! La tia curra'* is translated in the Prado manuscript caption as 'Oh! The bawdy old woman'.

p. 62 – *'Neither more nor less'*: *'Pinta un gorilla'* translates as 'paint a gorilla'.

p. 63 – *'Thou who canst not'*: the opening here echoes Allen Ginsberg's poem 'Song' from 1954, published in *Howl and Other Poems*, City Lights, San Francisco, 1956.

p. 64 – *'The sleep of reason produces monsters'* includes an echo of John Milton's 'On the Morning of Christ's Nativity'

("A Wakeful Trump of Doom Must Thunder the Valley Deep", published in *Poems of Mr. John Milton*, Humphrey Moseley, London, 1645).

p. 65 – *'They spin finely'*: *'y la trama'* translates as 'and the plot'.

p. 67 – *'Correction'*: *'Dies'* (from Latin, meaning 'Day of Wrath').

p. 69 – *'Tale-bearers – Blasts of wind'*: 'Śākyamuni' refers to another name for Buddha.

p. 71 – *'The Chinchillas'*: 'Spit fire. Spout rain.' is a quote from *King Lear* (Act 3, Scene 2) by William Shakespeare.

p. 72 – *'They spruce themselves up'*: In Norse mythology, 'Naglfar' is a boat made entirely from fingernails and toenails of the dead.

p. 74 – *'What a golden beak!'*: Bittacus refers to the nickname given to a variety of talking parrot introduced to the Roman court, by Ctesias in the fifth century BCE.

p. 76 – *'Until death'*: *'la madre de la muerte'* means 'the mother of death'.

p. 83 – *'Who would have thought it!'*: 'the *auri sacra fames*' (from Latin, meaning 'accursed hunger for gold'. As mentioned in Virgil's *Aeneid*, Book 3, 57).

p. 85 – *'Bon Voyage'*: 'If light thinks of time, darkness is time / thinking about itself'. This is a play on Octavio Paz's poem 'Draft of Shadows' which states: 'Light is time thinking about itself'.

p. 89 – *'Pretty teacher'* and p. 101 – *'It is time'* are dedicated to Sandeep Parmar.

104

p. 93 – *'You will not escape'*, p. 94 – *'It is better to be lazy'* and p. 96 – *'Can't anyone untie us?'* all refer to Salvador Dalí, whose amended versions of his personal manuscript of *Los Caprichos* were exhibited in León, Nicaragua in February 2017. The author also refers to Dalí by his unflattering nickname: Avida Dollars.

p. 97 – *'You understand?... well, as I say...'*: '¡Desgraciado *Almirante! Sangre y ceniza*' (Disgraced Admiral! Blood and ash) are lines taken from Ruben Dario's poem 'A Colón' (To Columbus), published in the Penguin edition, as mentioned above.

Biographical Note

JAMES BYRNE is a poet, editor and translator. His most recent poetry collections are *Everything Broken Up Dances* (Tupelo, 2015) and *White Coins* (Arc Publications, 2015). Other publications include *Blood/Sugar* (Arc, 2009), *WITHDRAWALS*, *Soapboxes* (both KFS, 2019 and 2014) and *Myths of the Savage Tribe* (a co-authored text with Sandeep Parmar, Oystercatcher, 2014).

Byrne received an MFA in Poetry from New York University, where he was given a Stein Fellowship ('Extraordinary International Scholar'). He was the Poet in Residence at Clare Hall, University of Cambridge. He currently lives near Liverpool where he is a Senior Lecturer in Creative Writing at Edge Hill University.

Byrne is renowned for his commitment to international poetries and poetics. He is the International Editor for Arc Publications and was editor of *The Wolf*, which he co-founded, from 2002-2017. In 2012, with ko ko thett, Byrne co-edited *Bones Will Crow*, the first anthology of contemporary Burmese poetry to be published in English (Arc, 2012). In 2017, with Robert Sheppard, he edited *Atlantic Drift*, a book of transatlantic poetry and poetics (Arc, EHUP). In 2019, he co-edited, with Shehzar Doja, *I am a Rohingya*, the first anthology of Rohingya poetry in English. Byrne's poems have been translated into several languages and his *Poemas Escogidos* (Selected Poems) was published in Spanish in 2019 by Buenos Aires Poetry (translated by Katherine M. Hedeen and Víctor Rodríguez Núñez).

John Kinsella has written that "James Byrne is a phenomenon and *Blood/Sugar* is astonishing... He is a complete original." Ishion Hutchinson wrote of *White Coins*: "this is language charged with a tough, sensual contraflow music, vividly alive to inquiry and witness [...] an astonishing work, one where virtù and gravitas are in concord with a hermetic passion, one fiercely and beautifully saying the unsayable."